Piano Accompaniment

Level 1

Alfred's
INSTRUMENTAL
PLAY-ALONG

EASY CHRISTMAS CAROLS
Instrumental Solos

Arranged by Bill Galliford, Ethan Neuburg and Tod Edmondson

ISBN-10: 0-7390-8401-1
ISBN-13: 978-0-7390-8401-4

Contents

AWAY IN A MANGER (MEDLEY)

Music by
JAMES R. MURRAY (1887) and
WILLIAM J. KIRKPATRICK

Slowly and gently (♩ = 84)

9 **"Away in a Manger"**
Music by JAMES R. MURRAY (1887)

Away in a Manger (Medley) - 5 - 1

29 **"Away in a Manger (Cradle Song)"**
Music by WILLIAM J. KIRKPATRICK

ANGELS WE HAVE HEARD ON HIGH

Traditional French Melody

Angels We Have Heard on High - 4 - 1

COME, THOU LONG-EXPECTED JESUS

Music by
ROLAND H. PRICHARD

Come, Thou Long-Expected Jesus - 5 - 1

GO, TELL IT ON THE MOUNTAIN

Traditional Spiritual

Go, Tell It on the Mountain - 3 - 1

Go, Tell It on the Mountain - 3 - 3

WE THREE KINGS

Words and Music by
JOHN H. HOPKINS, JR. (1857)

Moderately slow and tenderly (♩ = 180)
(♩. = 60 This represents the song pulse feel counted in one.)

We Three Kings - 6 - 1

We Three Kings - 6 - 2

22

IT CAME UPON THE MIDNIGHT CLEAR

Music by
RICHARD S. WILLIS

It Came Upon the Midnight Clear - 4 - 1

It Came Upon the Midnight Clear - 4 - 2

28

It Came Upon the Midnight Clear - 4 - 3

HARK! THE HERALD ANGELS SING

Music by
FELIX MENDELSSOHN

JOY TO THE WORLD

Music by
GEORGE F. HANDEL

Moderately slow and gentle (♩ = 72)

Joy to the World - 3 - 1

O COME, O COME, EMMANUEL

Music Adapted by
THOMAS HELMORE

O Come, O Come, Emmanuel - 4 - 1

O Come, O Come, Emmanuel - 4 - 4

SILENT NIGHT

Words and Music by
JOSEPH MOHR and FRANZ GRUBER

Silent Night - 4 - 1

O COME ALL YE FAITHFUL

Music by
JOHN FRANCIS WADE

O Come All Ye Faithful - 3 - 1

46

O LITTLE TOWN OF BETHLEHEM

Music by
LEWIS H. REDNER

O Little Town of Bethlehem - 3 - 1

O Little Town of Bethlehem - 3 - 3

THE FIRST NOEL

Traditional English Carol

The First Noel - 2 - 1

The First Noel - 2 - 2

WHAT CHILD IS THIS?

Old English Air

Moderately (♩ = 104)

What Child Is This? - 4 - 1

What Child Is This? - 4 - 2

INSTRUMENTAL SOLOS · VOLUME 1 & VOLUME 2

Rolling Stone® Magazine's "The 500 Greatest Songs of All Time" is the ultimate celebration of the greatest rock & roll songs of all time. The editors of *Rolling Stone®* called on a five-star jury of singers, musicians, producers, industry figures, critics and, of course, songwriters. The 172 voters, who included Brian Wilson, Joni Mitchell and Wilco's Jeff Tweedy, nominated 2,103 songs in virtually every pop-music genre of the past half-century and beyond, from Hank Williams to OutKast. The results were tabulated according to a weighted point system. Alfred is proud to introduce an impressive new instrumental play-along collections that make songs from the *Rolling Stone 500* playable to music makers everywhere!

Selections from *Rolling Stone®* Magazine's 500 Greatest Songs of All Time: Instrumental Solos, Vol. 1 & 2

Each book contains a carefully edited part that is appropriate for Level 2-3 players, and a fully orchestrated accompaniment CD that includes both demo and play-along tracks for each song. Vol. 1 titles: Both Sides, Now • Desperado • Everyday People • A Hard Day's Night • Honky Tonk Women • Moondance • (We're Gonna) Rock Around the Clock • Soul Man • When a Man Loves a Woman • and more. Vol. 2 titles: Blueberry Hill • Dancing Queen • Hotel California • How Deep Is Your Love • I Got You (I Feel Good) • In the Midnight Hour • (I Can't Get No) Satisfaction • Spirit in the Sky • You Send Me • and more.

VOL. 1	VOL. 2		
(00-30335)	(00-30842)	Flute (Book & CD)	$12.95
(00-30338)	(00-30845)	Clarinet (Book & CD)	$12.95
(00-30341)	(00-30848)	Alto Sax (Book & CD)	$12.95
(00-30344)	(00-30851)	Tenor Sax (Book & CD)	$12.95
(00-30347)	(00-30854)	Trumpet (Book & CD)	$12.95
(00-30350)	(00-30857)	Horn in F (Book & CD)	$12.95
(00-30353)	(00-30860)	Trombone (Book & CD)	$12.95
(00-30359)	(00-30866)	Violin (Book & CD)	$14.95
(00-30362)	(00-30869)	Viola (Book & CD)	$14.95
(00-30365)	(00-30872)	Cello (Book & CD)	$14.95
(00-30356)	(00-30863)	Piano Accompaniment (Book & CD)	$14.95